Joseph's Testament

JOSEPH'S TESTAMENT

of the first Christmas

Philip Robinson

ULSTER-SCOTS ACADEMY PRESS

First published in 2021 by the Ulster-Scots
Academy Press.

Philip Robinson © 2021

ISBN 978-1-9163758-5-7

Front cover image is of *St Joseph with Infant
Christ in his Arms* by Guido Reni (1635)

Back cover image is *Camels with a howdah*, by
Émile and Adolphe Rouargue (1855)

Contents

CONTENTS

Prelude

The two sides of the Christmas Story

The two certain, and possibly the only, witnesses of the actual birth of Jesus Christ in Bethlehem over 2000 years ago, were the baby's mother Mary and her husband Joseph.

In the Bible, there are only two of the four Gospel books that relate this 'nativity' story. First of all, in *The Gospel according to St. Matthew*, it is reported by the Apostle Matthew as it was remembered by Joseph, while in *The Gospel according to St. Luke*, the story is told by Luke as he received it (apparently) from the lips of Mary herself.

But it is the in last of the four Gospels – that is, *The Gospel according to St. John* – where we might have expected to find Mary's stories of Jesus's birth and childhood, for the author of this *Gospel* book was Jesus's 'beloved' disciple John, who, at the crucifixion was given sole responsibility by Jesus for the subsequent care of his mother:

> *"When Jesus therefore saw his mother, and the disciple standing by, whom he loved, he saith unto his mother, Woman, behold thy son! Then saith he to the disciple, Behold thy mother! And from that hour that disciple took her unto his own home."*

> (John 19: 26-27)

The later historical record places John and Mary in Ephesus (in modern Turkey) during the years of the early church there. It is in this location that Luke probably recorded the various 'sayings' and stories of Jesus as an infant and child, up to the age of 12 when he declared God, not Joseph to be his 'Father':

> *"Now his parents went to Jerusalem every year at the feast of the passover. And when he was twelve years old, they went up to Jerusalem after the custom of the feast. And when they had fulfilled the days, as they returned, the child Jesus tarried behind in Jerusalem; and Joseph and his mother knew not of it. But they, supposing him to have been in the company, went a day's journey; and they sought him among their kinsfolk and acquaintance. And when they found him not, they turned back again to Jerusalem, seeking him. And it came to pass, that after three days they found him in the temple, sitting in the midst of the doctors, both hearing them, and asking them questions. And all that heard him were astonished at his understanding and answers. And when they saw him, they were amazed: and his mother said unto him, Son, why hast thou thus dealt with us? behold, thy father and I have sought thee sorrowing. And he said unto them, How is it that ye sought me? wist ye not that I must be about my Father's business?"*

> (Luke 2: 41-49)

This story, and the others from Mary about the conception, birth, and childhood of Jesus that are all unique to

Luke's *Gospel*, culminate with the observation by Luke that *"his mother kept all these sayings in her heart"* (Luke 2: 50) and this would suggest that Luke heard them from Mary herself.

Luke was a recorder and reporter, but not an eye-witness, of any of the events in his *Gospel*. He was a Greek convert and a travelling helper and companion of the Apostle Paul on his missionary journeys around the Mediterranean. During these trips they visited Ephesus more than once (as recorded in Luke's other book in the New Testament, *The Acts of the Apostles*, and in Paul's *Epistle to the Ephesians*).

On the other hand, John in his own *Gospel* (written years later than Luke's) had nothing to add to the earthly events surrounding the nativity as described in the *Gospels* of Matthew and Luke. Instead John opens his *Gospel* with a spiritual and eternal perspective on the event, a perfect summary of the Divine significance of the nativity of the Son of God:

> *"In the beginning was the Word, and the Word was with God, and the Word was God. The same was in the beginning with God. All things were made by him; and without him was not any thing made that was made. … And the Word was made flesh, and dwelt among us, (and we beheld his glory, the glory as of the only begotten of the Father, full of grace and truth."*

(John 1: 1-3, 14)

The New Testament, as a whole, begins with Matthew's *Gospel*, and opens with words which (both in English and in the original Greek), have deep multi-layered meaning: *"The book of the generation of Jesus Christ, the son of David, the son of Abraham."* (Matthew 1:1)

The Apostle Matthew was from Galilee, a tax-collector (rather than a fisherman like most of the others), before abandoning his job and becoming one of the 'twelve' disciples to follow Jesus. But he was familiar with Joseph's family and occupation even at that time, and records the reaction of the locals when Jesus began his ministry in Galilee:

> *"And when he was come into his own country, he taught them in their synagogue, insomuch that they were astonished, and said, Whence hath this man this wisdom, and these mighty works? Is not this the carpenter's son? is not his mother called Mary? and his brethren, James, and Joses, and Simon, and Judas?"*
>
> (Matthew 13: 54-55)

Joseph appears to have died some time before, between the years when Jesus was 12 and 30, but his eldest genetic son, known as 'James the Just', became the leader of the first Jerusalem church after the Resurrection and Ascension of Jesus, and at a time when Matthew and the other Apostles were still in Jerusalem. It is also possible that some of the stories of the nativity events related by Joseph – *"a just man"* (Matthew 1: 19) – were reported to Matthew from his son "James the Just".

Fragment

Joseph's account of the Birth of Jesus

(Matthew 1: 18-25)

[18] Now the birth of Jesus Christ was on this wise: When as his mother Mary was espoused to Joseph, before they came together, she was found with child of the Holy Ghost.

[19] Then Joseph her husband, being a just man, and not willing to make her a public example, was minded to put her away privily.

[20] But while he thought on these things, behold, the angel of the LORD appeared unto him in a dream, saying, Joseph, thou son of David, fear not to take unto thee Mary thy wife: for that which is conceived in her is of the Holy Ghost.

[21] And she shall bring forth a son, and thou shalt call his name JESUS: for he shall save his people from their sins.

[22] Now all this was done, that it might be fulfilled which was spoken of the Lord by the prophet, saying,

23 Behold, a virgin shall be with child, and shall bring forth a son, and they shall call his name Emmanuel, which being interpreted is, God with us.

24 Then Joseph being raised from sleep did as the angel of the Lord had bidden him, and took unto him his wife:

25 And knew her not till she had brought forth her firstborn son: and he called his name JESUS.

Chapter 1

Joseph's 'Calling': His first encounter with the Angel of the Lord

Joseph's account of the nativity begins with his understandable reaction to the news that the girl he was about to marry was expecting a child, despite the fact that they hadn't yet 'been together'. His intention was to divorce – to end a marriage process that had already begun – but to do it privately to avoid Mary's disgrace. However, this plan was completely reversed when, in a dream, he had the first of a number of angelic visitations.

In this 'calling' of Joseph to be the parent, guardian and legal father of the expected child, the angel told Joseph that he was to marry Mary, for the baby she would have had been conceived by the Holy Spirit; that it would be a son; that he was to call the child JESUS (meaning 'saviour', 'deliverer', 'rescuer'); and that this name was to be given to the child because he would "save his people from their sins".

"Joseph, thou son of David, fear not to take unto thee Mary thy wife: for that which is conceived in her is of

the Holy Ghost. And she shall bring forth a son, and thou shalt call his name JESUS: for he shall save his people from their sins."

(Matthew 1: 20-21)

It is not clear at what stage of Mary's pregnancy that Joseph was told that she was expecting. Mary's own visitation from the Angel Gabriel announcing that she had been chosen by God to conceive the Christ-child by the Holy Spirit (as recorded in Luke's *Gospel*), and her acceptance of the role, obviously came first. The conception was quickly followed (on Gabriel's instruction) by Mary's trip to Judea to visit her elderly kinswoman Elisabeth, who was already six months pregnant with the future John the Baptist. Mary stayed with Elisabeth and her husband Zacharias for three months before returning to Nazareth in Galilee.

So, at some point during the first three or four months of Mary's pregnancy, Joseph was told of it and the substance of Mary's encounter with the Angel Gabriel, presumably from Mary herself. This then is the background to the message given by the Angel of the Lord to Joseph in his first dream.

Besides all the Old Testament prophesies that the Messiah or Christ would be a descendant of King David, there were others, including one that the child would be born to a virgin. In Matthew's account of this visitation from God to Joseph, he identifies and confirms one particular prophesy as being here fulfilled:

"Now all this was done, that it might be fulfilled which was spoken of the Lord by the prophet, saying, Behold, a virgin shall be with child, and shall bring forth a son, and they shall call his name Emmanuel, which being interpreted is, God with us."

(Matthew 1: 22-23)

This prophesy is found in the book of Isaiah, chapter 7, and was declared to the "house of David" by the then King of Judah, Ahaz:

"[1] And it came to pass in the days of Ahaz the son of Jotham, the son of Uzziah, king of Judah ... [13] And he said, Hear ye now, O house of David; Is it a small thing for you to weary men, but will ye weary my God also? [14] Therefore the Lord himself shall give you a sign; Behold, a virgin shall conceive, and bear a son, and shall call his name Immanuel."

(Isaiah 7: 1, 13-14)

The genealogy of Joseph given at the start of Matthew's *Gospel* has King Ahaz [Achaz] as the 6th generation in line from King David down to the Babylonian captivity in the 14th generation. As Joseph was a direct descendant of Ahaz, this prophesy could have been just as familiar to Joseph as his own genealogy was.

However, even with Joseph having a perfect trust in the 'Davidic Covenant' – that is the promise by God to King David that *"I will set up thy seed after thee, which shall proceed out of thy bowels, and I will establish his kingdom*

… and I will stablish the throne of his kingdom for ever"
(II Samuel, 7) – and knowing that Joseph himself was
placed in that very line of descent and promise, the real
dilemma for him may have been to reconcile this with
the later prophesy given to King Ahaz of a virgin birth
for the messiah.

But Joseph's immediate acceptance of, and subsequent
commitment to, the revelation from the Angel in his first
dream – that the baby was indeed the 'Son of God' – was
absolute. Both he, as the 'son of David', and Mary his
betrothed wife would now jointly parent the infant as their
own. They would indeed name him Jesus, and would raise
him in the knowledge and love of his heavenly Father.

Chapter 2

Joseph, the "son of David"

Joseph was not randomly chosen by God for this parental role. The first words addressed to him from God were: "Joseph, thou son of David," a title which was understood in his generation to be a 'messianic' one, applied to the promised Messiah or Christ in the shape of a future King – a descendant of King David to fulfil God's promises to him in the Old Testament of an anointed King who would establish the everlasting Kingdom of God on earth:

> "*12 And when thy days be fulfilled, and thou shalt sleep with thy fathers, I will set up thy seed after thee, which shall proceed out of thy bowels, and I will establish his kingdom. 13 He shall build an house for my name, and I will stablish the throne of his kingdom for ever.*"
>
> (II Samuel 7: 12-13)

Indeed, the 'genealogy' that immediately precedes Joseph's narrative in chapter 1 of Matthew's *Gospel* is explicitly that of Joseph, charting *his* (that is, Joseph's) descent from Abraham, Isaac and Jacob, though Judah and King David, and King Solomon:

*"¹ The book of the generation of Jesus Christ, the son of David, the son of Abraham. ² **Abraham** begat Isaac; and Isaac begat Jacob; and Jacob begat Judas [Judah] and his brethren;*

...

*⁶ And Jesse begat **David the king**; and David the king begat Solomon of her that had been the wife of Urias; ⁷ And Solomon begat Roboam; and Roboam begat Abia; and Abia begat Asa; ⁸ And Asa begat Josaphat; and Josaphat begat Joram; and Joram begat Ozias; ⁹ And Ozias begat Joatham; and Joatham begat Achaz; and Achaz begat Ezekias;*

...

*¹⁶ And Jacob **begat Joseph the husband of Mary**, of whom was born Jesus, who is called Christ."*

(Matthew 1: 1-2, 6-8, 16)

The Old Testament prophesies relating to God's promise that a descendant of King David would establish his throne (as an everlasting Kingdom with the Messiah exercising universal authority) was understood, in Jesus's generation, to mean that a long-awaited 'Son of David' would be proclaimed the Messiah-King in Jerusalem. So we find throughout Matthew's *Gospel* that Jesus is often addressed by the title of "Son of David", with the implied expectation that he was the Christ, born to be King, or at the very least, King of the Jews to deliver Israel from Roman rule and their 'puppet' Herodian kings:

> *"And when Jesus departed thence, two blind men followed him, crying, and saying, **Thou son of David, have mercy on us.**"* (Matthew 9: 27)

> *"And all the people were amazed, and said, Is not this **the son of David**?" (Matthew 12, 23)*

> *"And, behold, a woman of Canaan came out of the same coasts, and cried unto him, saying, Have mercy on me, **O Lord, thou son of David**; my daughter is grievously vexed with a devil."* (Matthew 15: 22)

> *"And, behold, two blind men sitting by the way side, when they heard that Jesus passed by, cried out, saying, Have mercy on us, **O Lord, thou son of David**."* (Matthew 20: 30)

The climax of this expectation was of course Jesus's triumphal entry into Jerusalem, days before his crucifixion, when he again was hailed as the 'Son of David':

> *"And a very great multitude spread their garments in the way; others cut down branches from the trees, and strawed them in the way. And the multitudes that went before, and that followed, cried, saying, **Hosanna to the son of David**: Blessed is he that cometh in the name of the Lord; Hosanna in the highest."*
>
> (Matthew 21: 8-9)

The use of this title in Jerusalem upset the religious leaders:

> *"And when the chief priests and scribes saw the wonderful things that he did, and the children crying in the temple, and saying, **Hosanna to the son of David**; they were sore displeased, And said unto him, Hearest thou what these say?"*

> (Matthew 21: 15-16)

However, it was not only the claim that Jesus was the 'Son of David' that resulted in his rejection by the Jewish religious leadership, a rejection that led rapidly to them demanding his crucifixion. It was mostly the assertion that he was not born of a human father at all, but was, literally, the 'Son of God'. What was Jesus's response? Surprisingly, it was to tell them that the Messiah, the Christ, could not be *simply* an 'offspring' of David, but one who had also *pre-existed* him!

> *"While the Pharisees were gathered together, Jesus asked them, Saying, What think ye of Christ? whose son is he? They say unto him, **The son of David**. He saith unto them, How then doth David in spirit call him Lord, saying, The LORD said unto my Lord, Sit thou on my right hand, till I make thine enemies thy footstool? If David then call him Lord, how is he his son? And no man was able to answer him a word, neither durst any man from that day forth ask him any more questions."*

> (Matthew 22: 41-46)

In exactly the same way, Jesus told the Scribes and Pharisees that he could not be a literal descendant of Abraham – that is, he told them that although Abraham was *their* '[fore]father', as for himself, he *pre-existed* Abraham also:

> *"Then said the Jews unto him, Now we know that thou hast a devil. Abraham is dead, and the prophets; and thou sayest, If a man keep my saying, he shall never taste of death.* **Art thou greater than our father Abraham, which is dead?** *and the prophets are dead: whom makest thou thyself? Jesus answered, If I honour myself, my honour is nothing:* **it is my Father that honoureth me; of whom ye say, that he is your God***: Yet ye have not known him; but I know him: and if I should say, I know him not, I shall be a liar like unto you: but I know him, and keep his saying.* **Your father Abraham rejoiced to see my day:** *and he saw it, and was glad. Then said the Jews unto him, Thou art not yet fifty years old, and* **hast thou seen Abraham?** *Jesus said unto them, Verily, verily, I say unto you,* **Before Abraham was, I am***."*

(John 8: 52-58)

Chapter 3

Jesus: The 'Son of David', *or* the 'Son of God'?

When this question was asked regarding Jesus by almost all the Jews of his generation as a binary choice (in physical terms), it was equivalent to saying he could not be the son of Joseph **and** the Son of God. But even at the age of 12 when Jesus had been 'lost' by his parents in Jerusalem, he reminded his parents that his real Father was God Himself. However, it is also clear that he, as a child, remained 'subject' to his parents while still a minor:

> *"And it came to pass, that after three days they found him in the temple, sitting in the midst of the doctors, both hearing them, and asking them questions. And all that heard him were astonished at his understanding and answers. And when they saw him, they were amazed: and his mother said unto him, Son, why hast thou thus dealt with us? behold, **thy father and I** have sought thee sorrowing. And he said unto them, How is it that ye sought me? wist ye not that I must be about **my Father's** business? And they understood not the saying which he spake unto them. And he went down with them, and*

*came to Nazareth, and was subject unto them: but his
mother kept all these sayings in her heart."*

(Luke 2: 46-51)

For his disciples to be unaware of the virgin birth of Jesus
during his lifetime (before the *Gospel* narratives of Matthew
and Luke were written) was one thing, but to deny it there-
after was (and is) to deny Jesus Christ as the Son of God.

In the *Gospel* of John, we have an unequivocal account
of Jesus Christ (The Word) as 'One with God' before creation, as the agent of creation, and as the one who (in Jesus
of Nazareth) 'became flesh'.

*"In the beginning was the Word, and the Word was
with God, and the Word was God. The same was in the
beginning with God. All things were made by him; and
without him was not any thing made that was made
… And the Word was made flesh, and dwelt among us,
(and we beheld his glory, the glory as of the only begotten
of the Father,) full of grace and truth."*

(John 1: 1-3, 14)

Years after John's *Gospel* was written, the elderly Apostle
John was given the vision from Jesus in heaven that is recorded in the last book of the New Testament, *Revelation*,
where the ascended Jesus is described as the "root" rather
than the "son" of David:

*"And one of the elders saith unto me, Weep not: behold,
the Lion of the tribe of Judah,* **the Root of David,**

hath prevailed to open the book, and to loose the seven seals thereof."

(Revelation 5: 5)

In the closing chapter of *Revelation* (and therefore the closing chapter of the whole Bible), Jesus proclaims his standing outside of linear time:

"I am Alpha and Omega, the beginning and the end, the first and the last."

(Revelation 22: 13)

Should there be any doubt that this meant he had fulfilled all the Old Testament prophesies concerning his divinity as the 'Son of God', *and* his humanity as the 'Son of Man' during his time in the world, he ends the whole Bible with a statement that he (eternally) is not only the 'root' (that is, the origin and source) of King David's genealogy but ALSO his 'offspring' (that is the embodiment and fulfilment of the Davidic Covenant as the 'Son of David'):

*"I Jesus have sent mine angel to testify unto you these things in the churches. **I am the root and the offspring of David**, and the bright and morning star."*

(Revelation 22: 16)

Fragment

The Wise Men from the East visit Bethlehem, and Herod's Slaughter of the Innocents
(Matthew 2: 1-23)

1 Now when Jesus was born in Bethlehem of Judaea in the days of Herod the king, behold, there came wise men from the east to Jerusalem,

2 Saying, Where is he that is born King of the Jews? for we have seen his star in the east, and are come to worship him.

3 When Herod the king had heard these things, he was troubled, and all Jerusalem with him.

4 And when he had gathered all the chief priests and scribes of the people together, he demanded of them where Christ should be born.

5 And they said unto him, In Bethlehem of Judaea: for thus it is written by the prophet,

6 And thou Bethlehem, in the land of Juda, art not the least among the princes of Juda: for out of thee shall come a Governor, that shall rule my people Israel.

7 Then Herod, when he had privily called the wise men, enquired of them diligently what time the star appeared.

8 And he sent them to Bethlehem, and said, Go and search diligently for the young child; and when ye have found him, bring me word again, that I may come and worship him also.

9 When they had heard the king, they departed; and, lo, the star, which they saw in the east, went before them, till it came and stood over where the young child was.

10 When they saw the star, they rejoiced with exceeding great joy.

11 And when they were come into the house, they saw the young child with Mary his mother, and fell down, and worshipped him: and when they had opened their treasures, they presented unto him gifts; gold, and frankincense and myrrh.

12 And being warned of God in a dream that they should not return to Herod, they departed into their own country another way.

13 And when they were departed, behold, the angel of the Lord appeareth to Joseph in a dream, saying, Arise, and take the young child and his mother, and flee into Egypt, and be thou there until I bring thee word: for Herod will seek the young child to destroy him.

14 When he arose, he took the young child and his mother by night, and departed into Egypt:

15 And was there until the death of Herod: that it might be fulfilled which was spoken of the Lord by the prophet, saying, Out of Egypt have I called my son.

16 Then Herod, when he saw that he was mocked of the wise men, was exceeding wroth, and sent forth, and slew all

the children that were in Bethlehem, and in all the coasts thereof, from two years old and under, according to the time which he had diligently inquired of the wise men.

17 Then was fulfilled that which was spoken by Jeremiah the prophet, saying,

18 In Rama was there a voice heard, lamentation, and weeping, and great mourning, Rachel weeping for her children, and would not be comforted, because they are not.

19 But when Herod was dead, behold, an angel of the Lord appeareth in a dream to Joseph in Egypt,

20 Saying, Arise, and take the young child and his mother, and go into the land of Israel: for they are dead which sought the young child's life.

21 And he arose, and took the young child and his mother, and came into the land of Israel.

22 But when he heard that Archelaus did reign in Judaea in the room of his father Herod, he was afraid to go thither: notwithstanding, being warned of God in a dream, he turned aside into the parts of Galilee:

23 And he came and dwelt in a city called Nazareth: that it might be fulfilled which was spoken by the prophets, He shall be called a Nazarene.

Chapter 4

Joseph and the infant King

Joseph's account of the nativity story in Matthew's *Gospel* is virtually silent for the months that pass between God's 'calling' to Joseph in chapter 1, and the arrival of the three Wise Men from the East to worship the child 'born to be king' in the next chapter. Chapter 1 ends:

> *"Then Joseph being raised from sleep did as the angel of the Lord had bidden him, and took unto him his wife: And knew her not till she had brought forth her firstborn son: and he called his name JESUS."*

> (Matthew 1: 24-25)

Then Chapter 2 begins:

> *"Now when Jesus was born in Bethlehem of Judaea in the days of Herod the king, behold, there came wise men from the east to Jerusalem, Saying, Where is he that is born King of the Jews? for we have seen his star in the east, and are come to worship him."*

> (Matthew 2: 1-2)

The familiar narrative of the stable birth and the visit of the Judean shepherds is left to Mary's account in Luke's *Gospel*.

Indeed, Joseph makes no mention of the stable birth, the baby in a manger, or the visit of the Judean Shepherds. In most people's mind, the nativity stories are 'merged' into a single narrative, but the visitation of the Wise Men from the East was some time later – not to a stable, but to a house; and *possibly* to a weaned infant rather than to a new-born baby. However, rather than creating a difficulty in reconciling the two accounts, they together provide a wholly harmonious and authentic record. It is as if the only records of any child's first years were described separately by mother and father – each with their own different memories of the same child.

It should also be noted that although the number of Wise Men (sometimes called 'Kings' or 'Magi') is now popularly taken to be three, but that is nowhere stated in the Gospels, only that there were three gifts brought.

Chapter 5

The origins of the Wise Men, and of their 'Wisdom'

"Now when Jesus was born in Bethlehem of Judaea in the days of Herod the king, behold, there came wise men from the east to Jerusalem, Saying, Where is he that is born King of the Jews? for we have seen his star in the east, and are come to worship him."

(Matthew 2: 1-2)

Where in the East did these Wise men come to Jerusalem from, and what was the source of their 'wisdom'? What caused them to observe a star as a significant 'sign' in the first place, and why did they interpret it the way they did?

The answers to these questions lie in those books of the Old Testament concerning the Babylonian exile that were written 500-600 years before the birth of Jesus. The 'exile' lasted about 70 years and started with a two-stage deportation – 597 and 587 BC. But only two generations later, it was reversed by a spectacular repatriation that included the rebuilding of the temple and city of Jerusalem – all sponsored and funded by order of the Persian King Cyrus the Great after his conquest of Babylonia in 538 BC.

The significance of this period of Jewish exile "by the rivers of Babylon", is highlighted in Joseph's genealogy at the beginning of Matthew's *Gospel*:

> *"And Jesse begat David the king; and David the king begat Solomon of her that had been the wife of Urias; And Solomon begat Roboam; and Roboam begat Abia; and Abia begat Asa; And Asa begat Josaphat; and Josaphat begat Joram; and Joram begat Ozias; And Ozias begat Joatham; and Joatham begat Achaz; and Achaz begat Ezekias; And Ezekias begat Manasses; and Manasses begat Amon; and Amon begat Josias;* **And Josias begat Jechonias and his brethren, about the time they were carried away to Babylon: And after they were brought to Babylon, Jechonias begat Salathiel; and Salathiel begat Zorobabel …"**

(Matthew 1: 6-12)

In fact, the whole genealogy from Abraham to Joseph and Jesus is summarised into three periods of 14 generations each with only this event identified outside of personal names:

> *"So all the generations from Abraham to David are fourteen generations; and from David* **until the carrying away into Babylon** *are fourteen generations; and* **from the carrying away into Babylon** *unto Christ are fourteen generations."*

(Matthew 1: 17)

From the perspective of the 'lineage' of Joseph's family history, the period of exile begins with the fate of Joseph's direct ancestor, Jehoiachin [spelled 'Jechonias' in Matthew], who was in fact the last individual in this genealogy to be King of Judah:

> *"And Nebuchadnezzar king of Babylon came against the city, and his servants did besiege it. And Jehoiachin the king of Judah went out to the king of Babylon, he, and his mother, and his servants, and his princes, and his officers: and the king of Babylon took him in the eighth year of his reign. And he carried out thence all the treasures of the house of the LORD, and the treasures of the king's house, and cut in pieces all the vessels of gold which Solomon king of Israel had made in the temple of the LORD, as the LORD had said. And he carried away all Jerusalem, and all the princes, and all the mighty men of valour, even ten thousand captives, and all the craftsmen and smiths: none remained, save the poorest sort of the people of the land. And he carried away Jehoiachin to Babylon, and the king's mother, and the king's wives, and his officers, and the mighty of the land, those carried he into captivity from Jerusalem to Babylon."*

> (II Kings 24: 11-15)

Two generations later, the grandson of the captive king Jehoiachin – Zerubbabel [spelled 'Zorobabel' in Matthew] – was chosen to lead the return of the exiles to Jerusalem as their 'Governor', with instructions to rebuild their temple and city, following the decree of King Cyrus of Babylon sanctioning this in 538 BC.

Progress on rebuilding the temple was slow, for the returned exiles had begun to neglect this duty in favour of building fine houses for themselves. However, the chastisement of the post-exilic prophets Haggai and Zechariah during the reign of Cyrus's successor in Babylon, King Darius, meant that work began anew, only to be objected to by Persian officials in Jerusalem who wrote to King Darius to complain and have the work stopped. A search of the Babylonian archives however, found the original order:

"Then Darius the king made a decree, and search was made in the house of the rolls, where the treasures were laid up in Babylon. And there was found at Achmetha, in the palace that is in the province of the Medes, a roll, and therein was a record thus written: In the first year of Cyrus the king the same Cyrus the king made a decree concerning the house of God at Jerusalem, Let the house be builded, the place where they offered sacrifices, and let the foundations thereof be strongly laid; the height thereof threescore cubits, and the breadth thereof threescore cubits; With three rows of great stones, and a row of new timber: and let the expenses be given out of the king's house: And also let the golden and silver vessels of the house of God, which Nebuchadnezzar took forth out of the temple which is at Jerusalem, and brought unto Babylon, be restored, and brought again unto the temple which is at Jerusalem, every one to his place, and place them in the house of God. Now therefore, Tatnai, governor beyond the river, Shetharboznai, and your companions the Apharsachites, which are beyond

the river, be ye far from thence: Let the work of this house of God alone; let the governor of the Jews and the elders of the Jews build this house of God in his place. Moreover I make a decree what ye shall do to the elders of these Jews for the building of this house of God: that of the king's goods, even of the tribute beyond the river, forthwith expenses be given unto these men, that they be not hindered. And that which they have need of, both young bullocks, and rams, and lambs, for the burnt offerings of the God of heaven, wheat, salt, wine, and oil, according to the appointment of the priests which are at Jerusalem, let it be given them day by day without fail: That they may offer sacrifices of sweet savours unto the God of heaven, and pray for the life of the king, and of his sons. Also I have made a decree, that whosoever shall alter this word, let timber be pulled down from his house, and being set up, let him be hanged thereon; and let his house be made a dunghill for this. And the God that hath caused his name to dwell there destroy all kings and people that shall put to their hand to alter and to destroy this house of God which is at Jerusalem. I Darius have made a decree; let it be done with speed. Then Tatnai, governor on this side the river, Shethar-boznai, and their com of the Jews builded, and they prospered through the prophesying of Haggai the prophet and Zechariah the son of Iddo. And they builded, and finished it, according to the commandment of the God of Israel, and according to the commandment of Cyrus, and Darius, and Artaxerxes king of Persia."

(Ezra 6: 1-14)

When the re-building and re-furnishing of Solomon's temple that had been destroyed and plundered by Nebuchadnezzar was finally completed in 516 BC, it established an *entente cordiale* between Babylon and Jerusalem while the Persian Empire held sway. Symbolic of this, Zorobabel's own name (given that he and his father Sheilteih were born and bred in exile) was Persian, meaning 'seed of Babylon'.

As far as Joseph's genealogy is concerned, his ancestors from King David down to Zorobabel are all well accounted for in Old Testament scripture. But from Zorobabel's son Abiud down to Joseph himself, not a single name in the lineage is recorded anywhere in the Bible, apart from the genealogy provided in Matthew 1: 13-16. The reason for this is simple: the last book of the Old Testament (Malachi) was written in the 5th century BC, and there is a long, 400-year gap between the post-exilic books of prophesy and the birth of Christ. During this 'gap' – sometimes called the 'blank page' in the Biblical record between the Old and New Testaments – the fulfilment of the messianic prophesies were studiously awaited by wise heads in Babylon, and passionately awaited by God-fearing hearts in Jerusalem.

The major prophet of the exile, Daniel, deserves special mention in the context of this Babylonian connection to the nativity story. The stories of his fearless refusal in Babylon to worship any other than the One True Living God, and his interpretation of Nebuchadnezzar's dreams may be among the most familiar stories of the Bible, but it is his prophesies relating to the first advent of Christ (in a predicted time scale extremely close to the actual) that connect immediately to the journey of the 'Wise men' to Jerusalem. As a man of righteousness, Daniel's standing was alongside that of Noah and Job:

> *"Son of man, when the land sinneth against me by trespassing grievously, then will I stretch out mine hand upon it, and will break the staff of the bread thereof, and will send famine upon it, and will cut off man and beast from it: Though these three men, **Noah, Daniel, and Job**, were in it, they should deliver but their own souls by their righteousness, saith the Lord GOD."*

> (Ezekiel 14: 13-14).

As far as Daniel's standing as a prophet of the first and second advents of Christ was concerned, this was confirmed by Jesus (significantly in Matthew's *Gospel*), when Jesus was asked about when the 'end time' would be. His response was:

> *"When ye therefore shall see the abomination of desolation, **spoken of by Daniel the prophet**, stand in the holy place, (whoso readeth, let him understand:) Then let them which be in Judaea flee into the mountains: Let him which is on the housetop not come down to take any thing out of his house: Neither let him which is in the field return back to take his clothes. And woe unto them that are with child, and to them that give suck in those days! But pray ye that your flight be not in the winter, neither on the sabbath day: For then shall be*

*great tribulation, such as was not since the beginning of
the world to this time, no, nor ever shall be.”*

(Matthew 24: 15-21)

Jesus was therefore pointing to the Book of Daniel, a particular scroll of the Old Testament written in exile in the
6ᵗʰ century BC, and copies of which were available both
in Babylonia and in Judea.

Daniel was one of a number of 'princes of Judah'
that had been brought to Babylon from Jerusalem by
Nebuchadnezzar for the express purpose of assimilating
them into his advisory court as 'skilful in all wisdom, and
cunning in knowledge':

*“In the third year of the reign of Jehoiakim king of
Judah came Nebuchadnezzar king of Babylon unto Jerusalem, and besieged it. And the Lord gave Jehoiakim
king of Judah into his hand, with part of the vessels
of the house of God: which he carried into the land
of Shinar to the house of his god; and he brought the
vessels into the treasure house of his god. And the king
spake unto Ashpenaz the master of his eunuchs, that he
should bring certain of the children of Israel, and of the
king's seed, and of the princes; Children in whom was no
blemish, but well favoured, and skilful in all wisdom,
and cunning in knowledge, and understanding science,
and such as had ability in them to stand in the king's
palace, and whom they might teach the learning and
the tongue of the Chaldeans. And the king appointed
them a daily provision of the king's meat, and of the wine*

*which he drank: so nourishing them three years, that at the end thereof they might stand before the king. **Now among these were of the children of Judah, Daniel, Hananiah, Mishael, and Azariah: Unto whom the prince of the eunuchs gave names: for he gave unto Daniel the name of Belteshazzar; and to Hananiah, of Shadrach; and to Mishael, of Meshach; and to Azariah, of Abednego.***"

(Daniel 1: 1-7)

But it was following Daniel's interpretation of Nebuchadnezzar's troubling dreams that the king made Daniel 'chief of the governors over all the wise men of Babylon':

*"The king answered unto Daniel, and said, Of a truth it is, that your God is a God of gods, and a Lord of kings, and a revealer of secrets, seeing thou couldest reveal this secret. **Then the king made Daniel a great man,** and gave him many great gifts, **and made him ruler over the whole province of Babylon, and chief of the governors over all the wise men of Babylon.** Then Daniel requested of the king, and he set Shadrach, Meshach, and Abednego, over the affairs of the province of Babylon: **but Daniel sat in the gate of the king.**"*

(Daniel 2: 47-49)

This then is the context of the Wise Men from the East coming to worship the child born to be King of the Jews.

Chapter 6

The Star of Bethlehem

It should be understood that the Babylonian 'Wise Men' over which Daniel had presided during the exile included 'magicians' and 'astrologers':

> *"There is a man in thy kingdom [Daniel], in whom is the spirit of the holy gods; and in the days of thy father light and understanding and wisdom, like the wisdom of the gods, was found in him; whom the king Nebuchadnezzar thy father, the king, I say, thy father, made master of the magicians, astrologers, Chaldeans, and soothsayers."*

(Daniel 5: 11)

Despite this background, the star that guided the Wise Men to Bethlehem was not simply interpreted by them as significant because they were astrologers. At first it had appeared to them in their own country in the East, and that was the very reason they gave in Jerusalem for undertaking a 3-4 month journey of hundreds of miles to find, and worship, the child 'that is born King of the Jews', and the star they had seen was described as 'HIS STAR':

*"Now when Jesus was born in Bethlehem of Judaea in the days of Herod the king, behold, there came wise men from the east to Jerusalem, Saying, Where is he that is born King of the Jews? for **we have seen his star in the east**, and are come to worship him."*

(Matthew 2: 1-2)

Another prophesy of a star to come 'out of Jacob' in the fifth book of the Old Testament is interpreted as referring to the first coming of Christ, with the sceptre referring to the second coming:

*"I shall see him, but not now: I shall behold him, but not nigh: **there shall come a Star out of Jacob**, and a Sceptre shall rise out of Israel, and shall smite the corners of Moab, and destroy all the children of Sheth."*

(Numbers 24, 17)

And in the last book of the New Testament, Jesus Christ refers to himself as the 'bright and morning star':

*"I Jesus have sent mine angel to testify unto you these things in the churches. I am the root and the offspring of David, and **the bright and morning star**."*

(Revelation 22, 16)

Chapter 7

A very different Jerusalem

The Jerusalem that the Wise Men entered after their three or four month journey from Babylon was a very different placc to the Jerusalem the Jewish exiles had returned to, and rebuilt, 400 years before. Judea's political and religious life had emerged from the 'intertestamental' period with a host of changes, perhaps best symbolised by the 'original' languages in which the Old and New Testaments were written (Hebrew and Greek respectively):

a. Language – Hebrew as the written language of Judea, outside of the religious context, was being replaced by Latin from the Roman administration, but already had been supplanted by Greek for non-religious education, culture and commerce. Although the original language of the Old Testament scrolls was of course Hebrew, a Greek translation of the Old Testament books, called the Septuagint, was compiled in the 2nd and 3rd centuries BC.

b. Temple – the second temple of the post-exile generation begun by Joseph's ancestor Zorobabel (replacing the first temple built by King David's son Solomon) had lasted from c.526 BC until it was destroyed by the Romans c. 70 BC. However the 'new' third temple built by the Roman vassal-King Herod was only completed in Joseph's generation.

c. The Throne of David – No descendant of King David was king of Judea or Israel during or after the intertestamental period. The Herodian dynasty, appointed by the Roman senate, had emerged during Joseph's generation and was not remotely Davidic.

d. Pharisees, and Sadducees – During the intertestamental period, two sects or schools of Jewish religious adherence emerged: the Pharisees, who were strict and obsessively controlling 'legalists', and the Sadducees who were theologically 'liberal' and often dismissive of 'supernatural' beliefs including resurrection.

e. The Jewish High Priesthood and Sanhedrin (Ruling Council) – When the Jewish ruling council of the Sanhedrin emerged, it was the Sadducees (small in number but closely allied to Herod), that held the residue of Jewish power and influence. In fact it was generally the case that Herod himself or the Roman Governors that chose the High Priest from among the ranks of the Sadducees.

f.   Changes in Jewish Religious life – During the intertestamental period the rival worship practices of the Jews and the Samaritans diverged, especially regarding the recognised place of the 'temple' for collective worship and observing festivals. For Jews, however, the most obvious 'new' feature was the local synagogue or 'meeting house' that enabled collective Sabbath worship of 10 or more households outside of the temple at Jerusalem. It is not clear when the synagogue emerged as part and parcel of Jewish observance, and may even have had its origins during the exile.

Chapter 8

Turmoil in Jerusalem

When the Wise Men reached Jerusalem, it seems the news of the birth of the Messiah that they brought was a source of great consternation to Herod and the chief priests and scribes, rather a cause of rejoicing. In the wake of their arrival, Herod questioned them 'diligently what time the star appeared', and then sent them on to Bethlehem to search for the child. After they left for Bethlehem, agitation and anxiety mounted back in Jerusalem. Herod 'was troubled, and all Jerusalem with him', and no wonder. Herod not only had built the temple that Jesus was eventually to enter many times, but he had appointed the High Priests and most of the Sanhedrin.

Bearing all this in mind, it comes as no surprise to learn that when the Wise Men came first of all to Jerusalem in search of 'he that is born King of the Jews', they ignored the sitting 'King of the Jews' and even the Jewish leaders in the temple. It was left to Herod to summon the High Priests and Scribes together and then ask the Wise Men to meet him privately. The Wise Men had slighted the Herodian dynasty and Herod the Great's own position as king. Indeed they had not sought an audience, but he had to summon them to him, and then pretend that he wanted to go and worship the child himself, if the Wise Men could find him.

> *"When Herod the king had heard these things, he was troubled, and all Jerusalem with him. And when he had gathered all the chief priests and scribes of the people together, he demanded of them where Christ should be born. And they said unto him, In Bethlehem of Judaea: for thus it is written by the prophet, And thou Bethlehem, in the land of Juda, art not the least among the princes of Juda: for out of thee shall come a Governor, that shall rule my people Israel. Then Herod, when he had privily called the wise men, enquired of them diligently what time the star appeared. And he sent them to Bethlehem, and said, Go and search diligently for the young child; and when ye have found him, bring me word again, that I may come and worship him also."*

(Matthew 2, 3-8)

Joseph's forefather King Jechonias, taken to Babylon with the captivity, was the last king of Israel or Judea in his line of ancestry from King David. When Jechonias's grandson, Zorobabel led the return from exile, he was only made a 'governor' of Judea under the Persian King.

For the greater part of the 400-year history of the inter-testamental period between the Old and New Testaments, the Persian Empire had been replaced by the Greek Empire, after Alexander the Great defeated the Persians in 313 BC. From this date, the Greeks' political and commercial control allowed their language and culture to get widely established, not only in Israel, but also across the 'known world' from Alexandria in Egypt to Babylon and beyond in the east. Greek political control did begin to disintegrate however in the 3rd century BC, with Israel coming under Egyptian control until 198 BC when Antiochus the Great of Syria conquered the region and divided the country into provinces. At this time, the provinces of Israel we are familiar with in the New Testament were set up: Galilee in the north, Samaria in the middle, and Judea in the south (including Jerusalem). There was a brief period of independence from 165 BC following the revolt of Judas Maccabeus until the Roman general Pompey's conquest of Palestine in 66 BC.

So it was only two generations before the Wise Men arrived in Jerusalem that Palestine had become part of the Roman Empire. The political context of the advent of Jesus Christ was one where the land was ruled by Roman governors and Roman-appointed Herodian kings.

At the time of the birth of Jesus (which is estimated to have been actually between 1 BC and 4 BC), Roman rule was exercised by Herod the Great who was the Roman vassal-King of Israel and Judea from 37 to 4 BC, and who's numerous but feuding offspring were to constitute a new Herodian dynasty.

Herod's father Antipater was an Idumean from the Negreb in the Edomite south of Palestine and was not considered a true Israelite even though his family had converted to Judaism. When the Roman general Pompey arrived in 66 BC, Antipater was an enthusiastic 'Jewish' supporter, and was rewarded by being appointed Procurator of Palestine, and in turn he appointed his 26-year old son Herod as governor of Galilee in 47 BC. Herod then made a name for himself by flushing out nests of Jewish brigands and putting them to death against the religious protocol of Jewish law, and in 40 BC, Herod was unanimously proclaimed King of Judea by the Roman senate. He ruled his subjects with an iron hand, constantly on the outlook for conspiracies against him, slaying numerous suspects even among his own friends and family.

Although King Herod was a ruthless leader, his Roman-backed power and resources enabled him to embark on a spectacular building programme that included several palaces, fortresses and the city-port of Caesarea complete with Roman temples and amphitheatre. But foremost among his building achievements was the 'third' temple in Jerusalem – rebuilt and enlarged by employing a thousand priests trained as masons, besides thousands of other workers. Begun in 20 BC it was barely completed in the days of Jesus Christ.

Chapter 9

The Wise Men see the Star again

Having left Jerusalem, the star appeared to the Wise Men again, and led them straight to the house where Joseph, Mary and the 'young child' were staying:

> *"When they had heard the king, they departed; and,* **lo, the star, which they saw in the east, went before them, till it came and stood over where the young child was. When they saw the star, they rejoiced with exceeding great joy.** *And when they were come into the house, they saw the young child with Mary his mother, and fell down, and worshipped him: and when they had opened their treasures, they presented unto him gifts; gold, and frankincense and myrrh."*

(Matthew 2: 9-11)

It was the same star that they had seen "in the east", but his time it was not celestial, but terrestrial.

Having left the darkness of Jerusalem's Vanity Fair, they once again 'saw the light'. The account of the nativity in John's *Gospel* speaks of Jesus coming in to the world as the light shining in darkness:

*"All things were made by him; and without him was not any thing made that was made. In him was life; and the life was **the light** of men. And the **light shineth in darkness**; and the darkness comprehended it not. ... That was the **true Light**, which **lighteth every man** that cometh into the world. He was in the world, and the world was made by him, and the world knew him not. He came unto his own, and his own received him not."*

(John 1: 3-5, 8-10)

Of course, later, during Jesus's ministry, he confirmed himself to be the "Light of the World":

*"Then spake Jesus again unto them, saying, **I am the light of the world**: he that followeth me shall not walk in darkness, but shall have the light of life."*

(John 8: 12)

But at the very time of the nativity in Luke's *Gospel*, when the Judean shepherds near Bethlehem had their visitation of the angel announcing the birth of Jesus, their vision began, literally, with a bright light, and 'the glory of the Lord shone round about them':

*"And there were in the same country shepherds abiding in the field, keeping watch over their flock by night. And, lo, the angel of the Lord came upon them, **and the glory of the Lord shone round about them: and***

they were sore afraid. And the angel said unto them, Fear not: for, behold, I bring you good tidings of great joy, which shall be to all people."

(Luke 2: 8-10)

Chapter 10

Joy to the World

The Wise Men's reaction to seeing the star again was not fear, but JOY. And this is the word that ends Joseph's account of the journey of the Wise Men to the infant Jesus in the first 10 verses of chapter 2 in Matthew's *Gospel*. What follows this first part of the chapter, in verses 11-13, are three of the most familiar verses in the Bible, and the climax of the nativity story told by Joseph:

> *"10 When they saw the star, they rejoiced with exceeding great joy. 11 And when they were come into the house, they saw the young child with Mary his mother, and fell down, and worshipped him: and when they had opened their treasures, they presented unto him gifts; gold, and frankincense and myrrh. 12 And being warned of God in a dream that they should not return to Herod, they departed into their own country another way."*

(Matthew 2, 10-13)

This second chapter of Matthew's *Gospel* is beautifully symmetrical, almost like some of the Psalms, with no mention of Joseph in the first 10 verses, as the course of the Wise Men's journey from the East in search of Christ is traced; then for the 3 central verses, we have the Joy of the 'Adoration of the Magi'; and then for the final 10 verses, the theme of Joseph's role as Jesus's protector from Herod is detailed. But what enormity of historical meaning is packed into these 3 short central verses!

The first thing to observe is that, unlike the shepherds, the Wise Men did not arrive on the night of Jesus's birth. It was a 'house' they entered, not an animal shelter with manger. There has been much debate about how old Jesus was at this point – ranging from a few days or weeks, to months, or even over a year. But regardless of the infant's age, the entire focus of the Wise Men was on the child and not the parents. Joseph is in fact, not mentioned when they entered and saw 'the young child with Mary his mother'. This contrasts with the arrival of the Shepherds in Luke's *Gospel* who *'came with haste, and found Mary, and Joseph, and the babe lying in a manger'*.

It is fairly obvious that Joseph spent time with the Wise Men before and after the 'Adoration', probably bringing them inside the house to *see the young child with Mary his mother'*. They also seem to have stayed the night nearby, for when they departed it was after being warned 'in a dream' to return to their own country 'another way'. The details of the Wise Men's journeys to and from Bethlehem could only have been learned for Matthew's *Gospel* from Joseph.

Chapter 11

The Gifts of Gold, Frankincense and Myrrh

We are not told in scripture that there were three Wise Men – there may well have been more – but there were three **gifts** that they brought as part of their worship. They had prostrated themselves in adoration of the infant, and, seemingly oblivious to the presence of his parents, presented the **child** with "*gifts; gold, and frankincense and myrrh*".

Almost universally in Christian commentaries, these gifts are interpreted as having a threefold significance: *Gold* – as a symbol of Christ's crowning as King; *Frankincense* – as a symbol of the precious ointment used for High-Priestly anointing (this anointing was to be actually performed by pouring such ointment on his head and feet at the beginning of his ministry, and also at the final week of his ministry by Mary of Bethany); and *Myrrh* – as a symbol of the balm to be used on Christ's death in the preparation of his body for burial (this usage of myrrh is recorded in John's *Gospel* by Joseph of Arimathea at Christ's burial following the crucifixion: (John, 19: 38-40).

The next thing we are told is that the Wise Men departed to return home, not via Jerusalem but by another way, having been *"warned of God in a dream that they should not return to Herod"*. That they had this dream confirms that the guidance of the star, and their whole journey, had been in obedience to God and not simply triggered by some Eastern wisdom. That we had these details recorded at all also confirms that the visit of the Magi was not a brief call at the door, lasting only a few minutes, but included a significant conversation with Joseph.

Chapter 12

Joseph's second dream and the flight to Egypt

"And when they were departed, behold, the angel of the Lord appeareth to Joseph in a dream, saying, Arise, and take the young child and his mother, and flee into Egypt, and be thou there until I bring thee word: for Herod will seek the young child to destroy him. When he arose, he took the young child and his mother by night, and departed into Egypt: And was there until the death of Herod: that it might be fulfilled which was spoken of the Lord by the prophet, saying, Out of Egypt have I called my son."

(Matthew 2: 13-15)

The Wise Men had just departed, having themselves been told in a dream by God not to return to Jerusalem and Herod, when Joseph was also warned by God in a dream of the real and immediate threat to the life of the infant Jesus from Herod. He was told to go immediately, so as soon as he arose from sleep in the middle of the night, he took Mary and the child Jesus and started out for Egypt.

As with Joseph's first dream, the second was also accompanied by a reference to an Old Testament prophesy. This time the prophet in question was Hosea rather than Isaiah:

> *"When Israel was a child, then I loved him, and called my son out of Egypt."*

> (Hosea 11: 1)

That these prophesies are flagged up as being here 'fulfilled' is an important thing to consider deeply. Hosea lived in the 8^(th) century BC in the northern kingdom of Israel, and he was commanded by God to *"Go, take unto thee a wife of whoredoms and children of whoredoms: for the land hath committed great whoredom, departing from the LORD."* His message to the people therefore would be from the heart – to speak against the idolatry and unfaithfulness rampant at that time.

The Israelites of Hosea's day were the descendants of the 12 sons of Jacob, who himself had been renamed 'Israel' by God. They were now described by God as an 'adulterous generation' and equated to an unfaithful wife, but one whom God would eventually bring back to Himself. Obviously, the 'historical' reference in Hosea 11: 1 was not to the future 70-year Babylonian exile and the exiles' return (as was most of the rest of his prophetic message), but, in this verse, to the earlier sojourn of the children of Israel in Egypt, and the calling back – the exodus – of the nation that had been cradled there back to the land promised to Abraham, Isaac and Jacob.

Interlude

The other (Old Testament) Joseph: Jacob's favourite son

"When Israel was a child"

The nation of Israel was called "my people" by God when speaking to the prophet Hosea, describing them as an "adulterous generation". Their idolatry and godlessness was equated to the adultery and resultant offspring of an unfaithful wife. Israel 'when a child' takes us back to the time when Jacob, along with 11 of his 12 sons and their families moved from Canaan to Egypt to live with Joseph, his long-lost favourite son. In total, this 'child' of a nation amounted to only 70 souls, but hundreds of years later, when the 'children of Israel' had been reduced to slavery by the Egyptians, it had grown to a massive nation at the time of the Exodus under Moses, with the 12 'tribes of Israel' descended from the 12 sons numbering 600,000 men (Exodus 12: 37).

"Then I loved him"

But 'Israel' was originally the name given to Jacob by God on his return from the East, now with his own young family, to his father Isaac and his birth-right in Canaan. On arrival in Canaan, Jacob had 'wrestled' with God, after which struggle he was told:

> *"Thy name shall be called no more Jacob, but Israel: for as a prince hast thou power with God and with men, and hast prevailed."*

> (Genesis 32: 28)

In all this, Jacob had God's singular favour over his brother Esau:

> *"Was not Esau Jacob's brother? saith the LORD: yet I loved Jacob, And I hated Esau, and laid his mountains and his heritage waste for the dragons of the wilderness."*

> (Malachi 1: 2-3)

"And called my son out of Egypt"

The prophetic reference in God's declaration to Hosea – referring to 'my son' rather than 'my people' – is the signal that bringing the Israelites out of captivity in Egypt back to the Promised Land of Canaan was to be seen as a foreshadowing of the return of the infant Jesus. But Jacob (Israel himself) was also 'called back' from Egypt to Canaan. And he alone 'returned' of the 70 or so of his family that had original settled in Egypt after Joseph had become Governor of Egypt under Pharaoh.

The return of Jacob from Egypt

When Jacob had been in Egypt for 17 years, and about to die, he made his favourite son Joseph swear that he would not be buried in Egypt, but that he would be taken back to his fathers' burial site in Canaan:

> *"And Jacob lived in the land of Egypt seventeen years: so the whole age of Jacob was an hundred forty and seven years. And the time drew nigh that Israel must die: and he called his son Joseph, and said unto him, If now I have found grace in thy sight, put, I pray thee, thy hand under my thigh, and deal kindly and truly with me; bury me not, I pray thee, in Egypt: But I will lie with my fathers, and thou shalt carry me out of Egypt, and bury me in their burying place. And he said, I will do as thou hast said. And he said, Swear unto me. And he sware unto him. And Israel bowed himself upon the bed's head."*

(Genesis 47: 28-31)

On receiving this promise, Jacob blessed Joseph, and also Joseph's two sons that had been born in Egypt. These two sons (Ephraim and Manasseh) were to receive Joseph's share of Israel's covenant inheritance in Canaan on an equal footing with Joseph's brothers. Here too, Jacob mentions that his most favoured wife Rachael, who was Joseph's mother, had died in childbirth. This was when giving birth to her only other son, Benjamin (Joseph's full brother), and she had been buried where she died, at

BETHLEHEM, where Benjamin was born:

> *"And Jacob said unto Joseph, God Almighty appeared unto me at Luz in the land of Canaan, and blessed me, And said unto me, Behold, I will make thee fruitful, and multiply thee, and I will make of thee a multitude of people; and will give this land to thy seed after thee for an everlasting possession. And now thy two sons, Ephraim and Manasseh, which were born unto thee in the land of Egypt before I came unto thee into Egypt, are mine; as Reuben and Simeon, they shall be mine. And thy issue, which thou begettest after them, shall be thine, and shall be called after the name of their brethren in their inheritance. **And as for me, when I came from Padan, Rachel died by me in the land of Canaan in the way, when yet there was but a little way to come unto Ephrath: and I buried her there in the way of Ephrath; the same is Bethlehem.**"*

(Genesis 48, 3-7)

When Jacob died, he was embalmed in the Egyptian manner reserved for nobility, and permission was given by Pharaoh for him to be carried out of Egypt back to Canaan with a "very great company" of chariots and horsemen:

> *"And Joseph commanded his servants the physicians to embalm his father: and the physicians embalmed Israel. And forty days were fulfilled for him; for so are fulfilled the days of those which are embalmed: and the Egyptians mourned for him threescore and ten days. And when*

the days of his mourning were past, Joseph spake unto the house of Pharaoh, saying, If now I have found grace in your eyes, speak, I pray you, in the ears of Pharaoh, saying, My father made me swear, saying, Lo, I die: in my grave which I have digged for me in the land of Canaan, there shalt thou bury me. Now therefore let me go up, I pray thee, and bury my father, and I will come again. And Pharaoh said, Go up, and bury thy father, according as he made thee swear. And Joseph went up to bury his father: and with him went up all the servants of Pharaoh, the elders of his house, and all the elders of the land of Egypt."

(Genesis 50, 2-7)

The return of the 'other' Joseph from Egypt

When Joseph, in turn, was about to die in Egypt, he made his brothers take an oath that his body also would be taken back to Canaan for burial. On his death, he too was embalmed after the manner of the Egyptians:

"And Joseph dwelt in Egypt, he, and his father's house: and Joseph lived an hundred and ten years. And Joseph saw Ephraim's children of the third generation: the children also of Machir the son of Manasseh were brought up upon Joseph's knees. And Joseph said unto his brethren, I die: and God will surely visit you, and bring you out of this land unto the land which he sware to Abraham, to Isaac, and to Jacob. And Joseph took an oath of the

*children of Israel, saying, God will surely visit you, and
ye shall carry up my bones from hence. So Joseph died,
being an hundred and ten years old: and they embalmed
him, and he was put in a coffin in Egypt."*

(Genesis 50: 22-26)

However, for hundreds of years, the embalmed body of
Joseph remained in Egypt until the time of the exodus of
the multitudinous nation of Israel. Then, and only then,
was Joseph carried back to Canaan in fulfilment of the
promise made to him:

*"And it came to pass, when Pharaoh had let the people
go, that God led them not through the way of the land
of the Philistines, although that was near; for God said,
Lest peradventure the people repent when they see war,
and they return to Egypt: But God led the people about,
through the way of the wilderness of the Red sea: and
the children of Israel went up harnessed out of the land
of Egypt. And Moses took the bones of Joseph with him:
for he had straitly sworn the children of Israel, saying,
God will surely visit you; and ye shall carry up my bones
away hence with you."*

(Exodus 13: 17-19)

Joseph the 'Dreamer' in the Old Testament

The life of Jacob's son Joseph in the Old Testament has often been described as a fore-shadowing or a 'type' of the life of Jesus Christ. And the role of dreams in this 'other' Joseph's life is interesting too.

Joseph's troubles began with his prophetic dreams:

"Now Israel loved Joseph more than all his children, because he was the son of his old age: and he made him a coat of many colours. And when his brethren saw that their father loved him more than all his brethren, they hated him, and could not speak peaceably unto him. And Joseph dreamed a dream, and he told it his brethren: and they hated him yet the more. And he said unto them, Hear, I pray you, this dream which I have dreamed: For, behold, we were binding sheaves in the field, and, lo, my sheaf arose, and also stood upright; and, behold, your sheaves stood round about, and made obeisance to my sheaf. And his brethren said to him, Shalt thou indeed reign over us? or shalt thou indeed have dominion over us? And they hated him yet the more for his dreams, and for his words. And he dreamed yet another dream, and told it his brethren, and said, Behold, I have dreamed a dream more; and, behold, the sun and the moon and the eleven stars made obeisance to me. And he told it to his father, and to his brethren:

and his father rebuked him, and said unto him, What is this dream that thou hast dreamed? Shall I and thy mother and thy brethren indeed come to bow down ourselves to thee to the earth? And his brethren envied him; but his father observed the saying."

(Genesis 37: 3-9)

Indeed, the young Joseph was called "the dreamer" by his brothers, and their jealousy of him was raised to such an intense hatred that they plotted to kill him. They cast him in a pit, but on the intervention of his brothers Reuben and Judah, he was instead sold for silver into slavery and taken to Egypt:

*"And when they saw him afar off, even before he came near unto them, they conspired against him to slay him. And they said one to another, **Behold, this dreamer cometh**. Come now therefore, and let us slay him, and cast him into some pit, and we will say, Some evil beast hath devoured him: **and we shall see what will become of his dreams**. And Reuben heard it, and he delivered him out of their hands; and said, Let us not kill him. And Reuben said unto them, Shed no blood, but cast him into this pit that is in the wilderness, and lay no hand upon him; that he might rid him out of their hands, to deliver him to his father again. And it came to pass, when Joseph was come unto his brethren, that they stript Joseph out of his coat, his coat of many colours that was on him; And they took him, and cast him into a pit: and the pit was empty, there was no water in it.*

And they sat down to eat bread: and they lifted up their eyes and looked, and, behold, a company of Ishmeelites came from Gilead with their camels bearing spicery and balm and myrrh, going to carry it down to Egypt. And Judah said unto his brethren, What profit is it if we slay our brother, and conceal his blood? Come, and let us sell him to the Ishmeelites, and let not our hand be upon him; for he is our brother and our flesh. And his brethren were content. Then there passed by Midianites merchantmen; and they drew and lifted up Joseph out of the pit, and sold Joseph to the Ishmeelites for twenty pieces of silver: and they brought Joseph into Egypt."

(Genesis 37: 18-28)

In Egypt, it was Joseph's ability to interpret the dreams of his first master, Potiphar, and then of Pharaoh, that eventually saw him rise to the highest position of governance in Egypt. The similarity of Joseph's elevation through his prophetic interpretation of Pharaoh's dreams, to that of Daniel in relation to King Nebuchadnezzar's dreams in Babylon over 2000 years later, is remarkable. But it is not only the events of Joseph's life, especially concerning his brothers' initial rejection of him, their attempts to kill, strip and throw him in a pit, and then to sell him as a captive slave to Egypt, that suggest parallels with Jesus' life and resurrection, but also the love and forgiveness that concludes the story.

"And when Joseph's brethren saw that their father was dead, they said, Joseph will peradventure hate us, and

will certainly requite us all the evil which we did unto him. And they sent a messenger unto Joseph, saying, Thy father did command before he died, saying, So shall ye say unto Joseph, Forgive, I pray thee now, the trespass of thy brethren, and their sin; for they did unto thee evil: and now, we pray thee, forgive the trespass of the servants of the God of thy father. And Joseph wept when they spake unto him. And his brethren also went and fell down before his face; and they said, Behold, we be thy servants. And Joseph said unto them, Fear not: for am I in the place of God? But as for you, ye thought evil against me; but God meant it unto good, to bring to pass, as it is this day, to save much people alive. Now therefore fear ye not: I will nourish you, and your little ones. And he comforted them, and spake kindly unto them."

(Genesis 50: 15-21)

A similar pattern of love, compassion and forgiveness on Joseph's part was displayed when his brothers first arrived in the cradle of Egypt ('*When Israel was a child*'):

"Then Joseph could not refrain himself before all them that stood by him; and he cried, Cause every man to go out from me. And there stood no man with him, while Joseph made himself known unto his brethren. And he wept aloud: and the Egyptians and the house of Pharaoh heard. And Joseph said unto his brethren, I am Joseph; doth my father yet live? And his brethren could not answer him; for they were troubled at his presence.

And Joseph said unto his brethren, Come near to me, I pray you. And they came near. And he said, I am Joseph your brother, whom ye sold into Egypt. Now therefore be not grieved, nor angry with yourselves, that ye sold me hither: for God did send me before you to preserve life."

(Genesis 45: 1-5)

Chapter 13

Safe in Egypt, but desolation in Bethlehem: The slaughter of the innocents

When the Wise Men had departed, Joseph arose from his second dream and took the infant Jesus and his mother Mary into Egypt. However, the scene in and around Bethlehem rapidly changed from one where Love and Life "came down" at that first Christmas, to a scene of hatred and death wrought by Herod. All children under the age of two in the district were slaughtered.

> *"Then Herod, when he saw that he was mocked of the wise men, was exceeding wroth, and sent forth, and slew all the children that were in Bethlehem, and in all the coasts thereof, from two years old and under, according to the time which he had diligently inquired of the wise men. Then was fulfilled that which was spoken by Jeremiah the prophet, saying, In Rama was there a voice heard, lamentation, and weeping, and great mourning, Rachel weeping for her children, and would not be comforted, because they are not."*

> (Matthew 2: 16-18)

The prophesy of Jeremiah 'fulfilled' here provides another link to the love and compassion of the Old Testament Joseph to his family, that is the first-generation 'children of Israel', for Rachael was the Old Testament Joseph's own mother.

> *"Thus saith the LORD; A voice was heard in Ramah, lamentation, and bitter weeping; Rahel weeping for her children refused to be comforted for her children, because they were not."*

> (Jeremiah 31: 15)

Although Rachel was birth-mother to only 2 of Jacob's 12 son's, she was the figurative 'mother' of all of them as she was not only the favourite and elevated wife, but the 'intended' before Jacob was tricked into marrying her elder sister Leah first. Leah was mother to 6 of Jacob's sons, including Judah and his first-born Reuben. Each of Leah's and Rachael's 'hand-maidens' bore 2 sons each to Jacob, while Joseph, Rachel's first-born, was younger than the others. Then last of all, when the family were on the move they came to Bethlehem and Rachel's next son, Benjamin was born. Tragically, Rachael did not survive herself, and Jacob buried her at Bethlehem, and erected a stone pillar there as a memorial:

> *"And they journeyed from Bethel; and there was but a little way to come to Ephrath: and Rachel travailed, and she had hard labour. And it came to pass, when she was in hard labour, that the midwife said unto her,*

Fear not; thou shalt have this son also. And it came to pass, as her soul was in departing, (for she died) that she called his name Benoni: but his father called him Benjamin. And Rachel died, and was buried in the way to Ephrath, which is Bethlehem. And Jacob set a pillar upon her grave: that is the pillar of Rachel's grave unto this day."

(Genesis 35: 16-20)

"And Jacob said unto Joseph, … And as for me, when I came from Padan, Rachel died by me in the land of Canaan in the way, when yet there was but a little way to come unto Ephrath: and I buried her there in the way of Ephrath; the same is Bethlehem."

(Genesis 48: 3-7)

This prophesy about Rachael "weeping for her children" – posthumously – and at Bethlehem where she died – is a poignant Biblical comment on the cruelty and murderous nature of this 'King of the Jews'. Herod died in Jericho very soon after, historians say about 4 or 1 BC, following an excruciatingly painful and putrefying illness known later as "Herod's Evil".

Chapter 14

The third dream of Joseph, husband of Mary: Called out of Egypt

The news of Herod's death, following the Slaughter of the Innocents in and around Bethlehem, came instantaneously to Joseph in Egypt through the third dream recorded in his testimony:

> *"But when Herod was dead, behold, an angel of the Lord appeareth in a dream to Joseph in Egypt, Saying, Arise, and take the young child and his mother, and go into the land of Israel: for they are dead which sought the young child's life. And he arose, and took the young child and his mother, and came into the land of Israel."*

> (Matthew 2: 19-21)

Herod had based his order to slay all children around Bethlehem that were 'two years old and under' on the likely age of the infant Jesus according to the time the Wise Men had said was the first appearance of the star in the East. The only thing that can be said with any degree of confidence about the age of Jesus at the time Jesus was 'called out of Egypt' by God is that he was no more than two years old at that stage, but possibly only a matter of months.

In any case, Joseph again followed God's instruction immediately and 'arose' taking Jesus and Mary back to Israel.

Chapter 15

The fourth dream of Joseph, husband of Mary: Return to Nazareth

"But when he heard that Archelaus did reign in Judaea in the room of his father Herod, he was afraid to go thither: notwithstanding, being warned of God in a dream, he turned aside into the parts of Galilee: And he came and dwelt in a city called Nazareth: that it might be fulfilled which was spoken by the prophets, He shall be called a Nazarene."

(Matthew 2: 22-23)

On the death of Herod the Great, the Herodian dynasty became somewhat fragmented. Caesar Augustus confirmed in Rome the dying wish of Herod that his kingdom be divided between three of his sons and installed Herod Archelaus as Ethnarch of Judea, Samaria, and Idumea; Herod Antipas as Tetrarch of Galilee and Philip as Tetrarch of the lands north and east of the Jordan.

Joseph's reluctance to return to Judea and settle there may have had as much to do with Herod Archelaus's power and authority being exercised from the capital city of Jerusalem, as any anticipated difference with Herod Antipas in Galilee in their respective capacities for cruelty. Regardless of his own view however, the instruction from God in Joseph's fourth dream was that he was to go on north to Galilee, to the town of Nazareth there where he and Mary had travelled from to Bethlehem right at the start: *"And Joseph also went up from Galilee, out of the city of Nazareth, into Judaea, unto the city of David, which is called Bethlehem; (because he was of the house and lineage of David:) To be taxed with Mary his espoused wife, being great with child."* (Luke 2: 4-5). And so the raising and nurturing of Jesus the Nazarene by Joseph and Mary could begin in earnest.

Epilogue

The other (New Testament) Joseph: Joseph of Arimathea

The physical growth of Jesus through his infancy from birth until he was able to fend for himself was a period during which God's provision of protection, nourishment and learning was delivered primarily by his mother Mary in some respects, and by Joseph in others. Joseph's role as a loving parent and guardian was an entrusted one, dependant on his obedience to God's direction and its delivery preordained according to prophesy.

But there was another period of Jesus's bodily presence on earth during which divine provision for his 'helplessness' was met by preordained human hands – in the first place this had been during his infancy, secondly at the time of his death and burial.

When Jesus breathed his last on the cross, and cried *"Father, into thy hands I commend my spirit"* (Luke 23: 46), another Joseph enters the scene. Joseph of Arimathea's role in attending to the spiritless body of Jesus is described in each of the four *Gospels*, each adding some information more than the others:

"When the even was come, there came a rich man of Arimathaea, named Joseph, who also himself was Jesus' disciple: He went to Pilate, and begged the body of Jesus. Then Pilate commanded the body to be delivered. And when Joseph had taken the body, he wrapped it in a clean linen cloth, And laid it in his own new tomb, which he had hewn out in the rock: and he rolled a great stone to the door of the sepulchre, and departed." (Matthew 27: 57-60)

"And now when the even was come, because it was the preparation, that is, the day before the sabbath, Joseph of Arimathaea, an honourable counsellor, which also waited for the kingdom of God, came, and went in boldly unto Pilate, and craved the body of Jesus. And Pilate marvelled if he were already dead: and calling unto him the centurion, he asked him whether he had been any while dead. And when he knew it of the centurion, he gave the body to Joseph. And he bought fine linen, and took him down, and wrapped him in the linen, and laid him in a sepulchre which was hewn out of a rock, and rolled a stone unto the door of the sepulchre." (Mark 15: 42-46)

"And, behold, there was a man named Joseph, a counsellor; and he was a good man, and a just: (The same had not consented to the counsel and deed of them;) he was of Arimathaea, a city of the Jews: who also himself waited for the kingdom of God. This man went unto Pilate, and begged the body of Jesus. And he took it

down, and wrapped it in linen, and laid it in a sepulchre that was hewn in stone, wherein never man before was laid." (Luke 23: 50-53)

"And after this Joseph of Arimathaea, being a disciple of Jesus, but secretly for fear of the Jews, besought Pilate that he might take away the body of Jesus: and Pilate gave him leave. He came therefore, and took the body of Jesus. And there came also Nicodemus, which at the first came to Jesus by night, and brought a mixture of myrrh and aloes, about an hundred pound weight. Then took they the body of Jesus, and wound it in linen clothes with the spices, as the manner of the Jews is to bury. Now in the place where he was crucified there was a garden; and in the garden a new sepulchre, wherein was never man yet laid. There laid they Jesus therefore because of the Jews' preparation day; for the sepulchre was nigh at hand." (John 19: 38-42)

From these four parallel accounts we are told that this Joseph came from Arimathea, a town in Judea, and that he was both a 'rich man' and a 'counsellor' (that is he was a member of the ruling Jewish 'Council' or Sanhedrin in Jerusalem). Only someone of Joseph of Arimathea's standing and influence could have had direct access to Pilate, the Roman Governor. For Joseph to be able to 'beg' Pilate for the body of Jesus on the early evening of the day of his crucifixion – and to negotiate this successfully – was remarkable. And given the role of the Sanhedrin in persuading Pilate to have Jesus crucified in the first place, it is also remarkable that a member of the Council would seek his body urgently before the approaching Sabbath evening.

But did this man believe that Jesus really was the Messiah? Joseph of Arimathea was not simply described as 'honourable', 'just' and 'a good man'; but he was also a 'disciple of Jesus' (albeit 'secretly for fear of the Jews'). He was said to be 'waiting for the kingdom of God', and despite being a Jewish Counsellor, he 'had not consented to the counsel and deed of them' in the crucifixion.

In John's *Gospel*, we find that when taking the body, Joseph was accompanied by another member of the Sanhedrin, Nicodemus, who we do know had been in private conversation with Jesus early on in his ministry. This conversation is probably one of the best-known in the Bible. And Nicodemus was then described as a 'Pharisee', 'a ruler of the Jews' and 'a master of Israel':

> *"There was a man of the Pharisees, named Nicodemus, a ruler of the Jews: The same came to Jesus by night, and said unto him, Rabbi, we know that thou art a teacher come from God: for no man can do these miracles that thou doest, except God be with him. Jesus answered and said unto him, Verily, verily, I say unto thee, Except a man be born again, he cannot see the kingdom of God. Nicodemus saith unto him, How can a man be born when he is old? can he enter the second time into his mother's womb, and be born? Jesus answered, Verily, verily, I say unto thee, Except a man be born of water and of the Spirit, he cannot enter into the kingdom of God. That which is born of the flesh is flesh; and that*

which is born of the Spirit is spirit. Marvel not that I said unto thee, Ye must be born again. The wind bloweth where it listeth, and thou hearest the sound thereof, but canst not tell whence it cometh, and whither it goeth: so is every one that is born of the Spirit. Nicodemus answered and said unto him, How can these things be? Jesus answered and said unto him, Art thou a master of Israel, and knowest not these things? Verily, verily, I say unto thee, We speak that we do know, and testify that we have seen; and ye receive not our witness. "

(John 3: 1-11)

The preparation of the body of Jesus for burial undertaken by Joseph of Arimathea and Nicodemus 'after the manner of the Jews' involved applying a mixture of myrrh and aloes and wrapping it in linen clothes with the spices. The application of myrrh on burial is a strong reminder of the third gift brought by the Wise Men and presented to the infant Jesus at Bethlehem.

Joseph then took the prepared and linen-clad body of Jesus and laid it in a sepulchre that was his own; a new tomb he had hewn out of the rock 'wherein was never man yet laid'. John's *Gospel* tells us that the sepulchre was 'nigh at hand' ... 'in the place where he was crucified'. With this work completed, Joseph 'rolled a great stone to the door of the sepulchre, and departed,' and Pilate ordered an armed guard be placed at the stone door.

All the things that Joseph did with the lifeless body of Jesus were necessary for the fulfilment of prophesy and the resurrection promise. There were many other Old

Testament prophesies fulfilled at the time of the crucifixion, but when that of Isaiah in chapter 53 verse 9 is
considered, one prophesy stands out – Christ making his
grave with the wicked [at the site of criminal execution]
and with the rich [in the rich man's tomb] in his death.

> *"He is despised and rejected of men; a man of sorrows,
> and acquainted with grief: and we hid as it were our
> faces from him; he was despised, and we esteemed him
> not. Surely he hath borne our griefs, and carried our
> sorrows: yet we did esteem him stricken, smitten of God,
> and afflicted. But he was wounded for our transgressions,
> he was bruised for our iniquities: the chastisement of our
> peace was upon him; and with his stripes we are healed.
> All we like sheep have gone astray; we have turned every
> one to his own way; and the LORD hath laid on him
> the iniquity of us all. He was oppressed, and he was
> afflicted, yet he opened not his mouth: he is brought as a
> lamb to the slaughter, and as a sheep before her shearers
> is dumb, so he openeth not his mouth. He was taken
> from prison and from judgment: and who shall declare
> his generation? for he was cut off out of the land of the
> living: for the transgression of my people was he stricken.
> **And he made his grave with the wicked, and with
> the rich in his death**; because he had done no violence,
> neither was any deceit in his mouth."*

(Isaiah 53: 3-9)

God's pre-ordained provision for the lifeless body of the
crucified Jesus through Joseph of Arimathea, and for the

helpless infant Jesus through Joseph the husband of Mary, gives us – in the testimony of these two Josephs – a wonderful picture of the timeless nature of God's providence from the beginning to the end.

Postscript

Whatever happened to Joseph?

In the Biblical record, the last reference to Joseph being still alive is when Jesus was 12 years of age. In Luke's *Gospel* we learn that Joseph and Mary went from Nazareth to Jerusalem every year at the time of the Passover, and Jesus with them. When Jesus was 12 years old, with Jesus inadvertently left behind, his parents returned to the temple where they found him among the religious leaders, asking and answering questions. His mother Mary asked him why he had done this to them, as 'thy father and I have sought thee sorrowing'.

> *"Now his parents went to Jerusalem every year at the feast of the passover. And when he was twelve years old, they went up to Jerusalem after the custom of the feast. And when they had fulfilled the days, as they returned, the child Jesus tarried behind in Jerusalem; and Joseph and his mother knew not of it. But they, supposing him to have been in the company, went a day's journey; and they sought him among their kinsfolk and acquaintance. And when they found him not, they turned back again to Jerusalem, seeking him. And it came to pass, that after three days they found him in the temple, sitting in the*

midst of the doctors, both hearing them, and asking them questions. And all that heard him were astonished at his understanding and answers. And when they saw him, they were amazed: and his mother said unto him, Son, why hast thou thus dealt with us? behold, thy father and I have sought thee sorrowing. And he said unto them, How is it that ye sought me? wist ye not that I must be about my Father's business? And they understood not the saying which he spake unto them. And he went down with them, and came to Nazareth, and was subject unto them: but his mother kept all these sayings in her heart."

(Luke 2: 41-51)

The significance of this 'last' reference to Joseph is enormous. When the 12-year old Jesus was challenged by his mother in the temple for being inconsiderate (as she saw it, but with particular reference to his distressed 'father'), he replied with what amounted to a counter-reprimand. His 'father's business' was not Joseph's, but God's, and they, of all people, should have understood that. Nevertheless, after this, they all returned to Nazareth, where Jesus was obedient to his parents Mary and Joseph for an unspecified time.

If Joseph almost completely disappears from the Biblical record after the childhood of Jesus, it is true that, similarly, we know almost nothing of Jesus during the years when he was a youth either, except that he continued to live with his family, in Nazareth, later becoming known as 'Jesus the Nazarene', and 'Jesus of Nazareth'.

Nazareth was in the northern province of Galilee, about

half-way between the Mediterranean coast and the shores of the Sea of Galilee. It is where Jesus began his ministry immediately after his baptism in the Jordan by John the Baptist and his 40-day 'temptation' in the wilderness: *"And he came to **Nazareth, where he had been brought up**: and, as his custom was, he went into the synagogue on the sabbath day, and stood up for to read."* (Luke 4: 16). There is an opinion among some that the term 'Nazarene' was derogatory, indicating that the place was generally despised among Jews. Indeed when Jesus called his first six disciples (all from Galilee), among them was Nathaniel who was from the neighbouring town of Cana (John, 21: 2). Nathaniel's reaction to hearing that Jesus was from Nazareth was typical:

> *"Philip findeth Nathanael, and saith unto him, We have found him, of whom Moses in the law, and the prophets, did write, Jesus of Nazareth, the son of Joseph. And Nathanael said unto him, Can there any good thing come out of Nazareth? Philip saith unto him, Come and see."*

> (John 1: 45-46).

Not only was it surprising that the Messiah could come from such a place as Nazareth, but to be identified as 'Jesus, son of Joseph' sounded just as incredible, as Joseph was not believed to be anything more than a lowly workman:

> *"And when he [Jesus] was come into his own country, he taught them in their synagogue, insomuch that they were astonished, and said, Whence hath this man this*

wisdom, and these mighty works? **Is not this the carpenter's son?** *is not his mother called Mary? and his brethren, James, and Joses, and Simon, and Judas? And his sisters, are they not all with us? Whence then hath this man all these things?"*

(Matthew 13: 54-56).

The parallel text from Mark's *Gospel* identifies Jesus as also a 'carpenter' (the word used in the original Greek, *tektōn*, is thought to have a more general meaning like 'builder', just as likely to be working with stone as wood). From these verses we understand that Jesus as a young man had followed and been trained by his 'father' Joseph in this occupation:

"And he went out from thence, and came into his own country; and his disciples follow him. And when the sabbath day was come, he began to teach in the synagogue: and many hearing him were astonished, saying, From whence hath this man these things? and what wisdom is this which is given unto him, that even such mighty works are wrought by his hands? **Is not this the carpenter, the son of Mary,** *the brother of James, and Joses, and of Juda, and Simon? and are not his sisters here with us? And they were offended at him."*

(Mark 6: 1-3)

But by the time Jesus began his ministry in Galilee, when he was aged about 30, it has to be assumed that Joseph had died. The account of the 'wedding at Cana' is the first of many examples of when Joseph is conspicuous by his absence.

The wedding at Cana was the scene of Jesus's first miracle, and his first disciples had been invited, along with his mother Mary and his 'brothers'. It was clearly a family affair and Mary appears to have had a significant place in the arrangements. We are not told whose wedding it was, but it may have been one of Jesus's siblings. The new and latest disciple of Jesus, Nathaniel of Cana, who was also present may also have been 'connected' in some way:

"And the third day there was a marriage in Cana of Galilee; and the mother of Jesus was there: And both Jesus was called, and his disciples, to the marriage. And when they wanted wine, the mother of Jesus saith unto him, They have no wine. Jesus saith unto her, Woman, what have I to do with thee? mine hour is not yet come. His mother saith unto the servants, Whatsoever he saith unto you, do it. And there were set there six waterpots of stone, after the manner of the purifying of the Jews, containing two or three firkins apiece. Jesus saith unto them, Fill the waterpots with water. And they filled them up to the brim. And he saith unto them, Draw out now, and bear unto the governor of the feast. And they bare it. When the ruler of the feast had tasted the water that was made wine, and knew not whence it was: (but the servants which drew the water knew;) the governor of the feast called the bridegroom, And saith unto him, Every man at the beginning doth set forth good wine; and when men have well drunk, then that which is

worse: but thou hast kept the good wine until now. This beginning of miracles did Jesus in Cana of Galilee, and manifested forth his glory; and his disciples believed on him. After this he went down to Capernaum, he, and his mother, and his brethren, and his disciples: and they continued there not many days."

(John 2: 1-12)

Perhaps overshadowed by the miracle of turning water into wine is the significance of the conversation between Jesus and his mother Mary. When she came to Jesus to tell him the gathering had run out of wine, his answer was a sharpish, *"Woman, what have I to do with thee?"*

Nowhere in the Bible does Jesus address Joseph as "father", nor Mary as "mother". Even on the cross when speaking to the apostle John and to Mary, Jesus had said *"unto his mother, **Woman**, behold thy son! Then saith he to the disciple, Behold **thy mother!**"* This point is nowhere more evident, nor better explained, than on the occasion when Mary and Jesus's brothers attempted to see Jesus while he was teaching his disciples:

"While he yet talked to the people, behold, his mother and his brethren stood without, desiring to speak with him. Then one said unto him, Behold, thy mother and thy brethren stand without, desiring to speak with thee. But he answered and said unto him that told him, Who is my mother? and who are my brethren? And he stretched forth his hand toward his disciples, and said, Behold my mother and my brethren! For whosoever shall

do the will of my Father which is in heaven, the same is my brother, and sister, and mother."

(Matthew 12: 46-50)

Clearly, given the childhood obedience of Jesus to his parents, these references cannot be taken as contradictory to the 5th commandment to *"Honour thy father and thy mother: that thy days may be long upon the land which the LORD thy God giveth thee"* (Exodus 20: 12), but they are, in their full and deep meaning, complementary obligations.

But once again, Jesus describes God as his Father, and that his mother and brothers are *"whosoever shall do the will of my Father which is in heaven."* And added to this, we have the injunction of Jesus to 'call no man your father upon the earth':

"And call no man your father upon the earth: for one is your Father, which is in heaven."

(Matthew 23: 9)

Joseph the 'Silent Witness'

The 'silence of Joseph' is a term applied by some today to the absence of any reference in the Bible to the death of Joseph. But others have observed that there is no mention of Joseph speaking either. Even when Joseph and Mary had been searching Jerusalem for the missing 12-year-old Jesus, and found him in the temple 'about his Father's business', it was Mary who spoke to their son of his father's distress.

From Matthew's *Gospel* we know something of Joseph's thoughts, intentions, actions and his reactions, but not of a single word spoken. We know of four dreams where he was spoken to by God, and in every case he simply 'arose' and obeyed. Mary, of course, spoke back to God and asked 'how can I …?' when told she would have a child. Moses when called by God asked how he could go to Pharaoh when he had a speech impediment. Zacharias, the father of John the Baptist, was even struck dumb when he questioned God's ability to give him a son because of the age of his wife Elisabeth and himself, remaining unable to talk until the time John the Baptist was born.

The silence of Joseph in response to God's call was a measure of his absolute faith and unquestioning obedience. It was also a reflection of his self-sacrifice and self-denial. Apart from Jesus, no-one in Joseph's day had a nobler birth-right, but humbler station in life. The silence of Joseph is a perfect example of the maxim about humility taught by Jesus when he commanded his followers:

> *"And call no man your father upon the earth: for one is your Father, which is in heaven. Neither be ye called masters: for one is your Master, even Christ. But he that is greatest among you shall be your servant. And* ***whosoever shall exalt himself shall be abased; and he that shall humble himself shall be exalted.***"*

(Matthew 23: 9-12)

The testament of Joseph is about his sacrificial service and complete obedience to God's will and purpose regarding the nurturing of **His** son. It is all about Jesus. Precisely how and when Joseph died is of no more import than the same unanswered questions about Mary.

Joseph's testimony tells of one mortal's God-forged link in the temporal chain that is **His**-story.

www.ingramcontent.com/pod-product-compliance
Lightning Source LLC
Chambersburg PA
CBHW061750050726
47598CB00002B/679